Original title:
I Didn't Sign Up for This Frost

Copyright © 2024 Creative Arts Management OÜ
All rights reserved.

Author: Rory Fitzgerald
ISBN HARDBACK: 978-9916-94-300-7
ISBN PAPERBACK: 978-9916-94-301-4

Unraveling in the Thaw

Snowflakes dance like tiny sprites,
Yet beneath, my plants miss the lights.
Roses confused in winter's reign,
They twitch and shudder from the strain.

In my sweater, I'm stuck like glue,
With socks that match, isn't that blue?
My coffee's cold, it's really absurd,
Why am I outside? Haven't you heard?

The Unexpected Beauty of Icy Resilience.

The garden gnomes are frosted white,
They smile, though their day is slight.
With ice on branches, the world's a mess,
Grass in a slumber, I must confess.

Birds in beanies, so quirky and neat,
Chirping a tune in snow-covered feet.
Nature's art's bold, without a doubt,
I'm just trying to figure it out!

Chill of Unforeseen Seasons

In flip-flops, I ventured outside,
But snowbanks mocked my sunny pride.
My toes are squished in frosty despair,
While squirrels laugh, thinking it's fair.

My mittens are lost; where could they be?
In the pockets of my sold-out tea?
The air bites back with an icy grin,
Why, oh why, did I let winter win?

Unexpected Glimmers in the Cold

Icicles dangle, like daggers of glass,
While I slip and slide, oh what a class!
The cats have made snow their favorite stage,
Bounding around like they're filled with rage.

Hot cocoa spills, what a lovely sight,
Sprinkles of chaos make it alright.
Winter's a prankster, it seems to insist,
On laughter and joy in a frosty twist.

Frostbitten Dreams of Summer

My sun hat shivers in the cold,
The beach ball's lost, its story told.
A popsicle left on the porch, alone,
Feels like summer's long-lost phone.

Flip-flops frozen on the mat,
Suncream now a snowball spat.
Sunscreen's cry, 'What have we done?'
Chasing snowflakes in the sun?

Whispers Beneath the Ice

Snowflakes gossip, soft and light,
'Who ordered this chilly plight?'
Icicles hang like pesky spies,
While penguins wear their winter ties.

Frosty whispers fill the air,
As snowmen laugh without a care.
They say spring's just playing coy,
Hiding behind the winter frosty toy.

The Unexpected Shiver

A warm drink's turned into a slip,
My sweater's waving a white flag trip.
Hot cocoa's frozen in my cup,
While snowflakes giggle and build up.

Socks mismatched, what a sight,
Ice cubes waltzing on the night.
That blanket fort I built with cheer,
Might just be a winter veneer.

When Winter Crashes the Party

We set the table for summer fun,
Then snowstorms joined the crazy run.
Hot dogs wearing blankets, oh dear,
Winter's humor brings the cheer!

The beach towels lost to snowdrifts high,
While snowflakes twirl as the guests sigh.
Laughter ringing through the frost,
In winter's jest, we laugh, not lost.

Frost-Streaked Memories

In the morning light, I slip and slide,
My coffee cup winks, it's winter's pride.
Socks that match? A distant dream,
As snowflakes giggle, plot a big scheme.

My pet cat laughs, she's warm and snug,
While I chase ice like a hapless bug.
Frozen branches wave 'hello' to me,
"We're cozy here, come join the spree!"

Embracing a Bitter Chill

The thermostat's set to nuclear heat,
Yet frostbite creeps on my frosty feet.
A scarf wrapped tight feels more like a hug,
While I dance with a snowman—quite the thug.

Each sneeze is a symphony, loud and clear,
As ice cubes assault my mug with cheer.
A sled ride? Oh, what a wicked twist,
Just me, my ego, and a bitter mist!

The Hasty Dance of Winter's Kiss

With slippery shoes, I twirl and glide,
Fall on my butt—oh, what a ride!
An igloo made of dreams and wishes,
Hopes drown in puddles, splashed by fishes.

Old man winter shuffles with flair,
While I question why I even care.
But laughter bubbles, in flakes it swirls,
As my next slip sends me into twirls!

Fractured Dreams Beneath Ice

My dreams were sunny, now frozen tight,
Each morning's battle—a chuckle in spite.
The air's a punchline, sharp and bold,
While I wrap up warm, feeling old.

Kids throw snowballs with laughter bright,
While I aim for glory, but lose the fight.
A winter wonderland, I'm quite the clown,
As frost-bitten feet bring me crashing down!

Captured by Coldness

The morning sun's a distant wish,
With blankets piled, oh what a swish!
A cup of cocoa seems so far,
While stepping outside feels like war.

My hair's a tangled, frosty mess,
Each breath a cloud—oh, what a stress!
Socks mismatched in this icy plight,
I swear I signed up for sunlight!

The Hardness of Unexpected Ice

I ventured out to greet the day,
But slipped and slid in a comical way.
With arms flailing, a graceful dance,
Turns out ice is not for romance!

My backside learns the frozen floor,
Grinning neighbors watch and roar.
I hope this fall's not on the news,
Just add it to my daily bruises!

Treading on Frosty Paths

Each step I take, a crunching sound,
Like munching snacks on snowy ground.
But what's this feeling? Tasty treats?
Nope, just ice beneath my feet!

Snowflakes whisper, "Take it slow,"
While my boots scream, "Let's go, let's go!"
In this ballet of slips and slides,
The winter's charm is where fun hides!

The Dilemma of Snowy Silence

The world is blanketed in white,
But still, I roam with sheer delight.
Yet every step's a drama queen,
With each fall, I'm a slapstick scene!

The snowball fight was where I thrived,
Yet being hit's how I survived!
With snowflakes falling all around,
I ponder if I'm glory-bound.

When Sunlight Becomes an Illusion

The sun peeks out, oh what a tease,
Warming my heart, but chilling my knees.
I planned for rays, not icy winds,
My dreams of tan, now frozen sins.

I wore my shorts, a beachy vibe,
But winter laughed, oh what a bribe!
Snowflakes danced like jolly jesters,
While I slip-slid like one of their testers.

Beneath Frost's Heavy Cloak

Dressed in layers, a marshmallow look,
Thought I'd be cozy, like a storybook.
But frostbite chuckled, a mischievous friend,
Who knew my smile would soon descend!

Each step I take, a comic scene,
Like Bambi's first walk on ice so mean.
Sliding, gliding, oh what a sight,
Winter's prankster, steals my delight.

Crystalline Secrets of a Cold Night

Stars like ice, twinkling on high,
Whispers of cold make me sigh.
I dream of summer, sun, and fun,
Yet here I am, with snowflakes spun.

Frosty secrets wrapped tight in night,
Jokes of warmth seem out of sight.
But hey, what's this? A snowball fight!
Laughter escapes, my spirits alight.

Whispers of Ice in the Silence

In the quiet, ice tries to creep,
Each crunch beneath feels like a leap.
Nature's giggles hide in the chill,
As I wobble past with comic skill.

Beneath the moon, the cold's embrace,
Turns my brisk walk to a clumsy race.
Yet here I stand, despite the frost,
Finding joy in laughter, not at all lost.

The Icebound Heart's Dilemma

Oh dear, my heart's turned to ice,
It makes for a poor romance advice.
Chilling moments, a frosty scene,
My love life needs a warmer routine.

Snowflakes dance on a frozen lake,
A warm hug is all that I make.
But alas, it seems rather absurd,
When my love feels like a popsicle served.

In thermal layers, I find my glee,
But when I try to dance, oh woe is me!
My two left feet on this slippery floor,
I'd rather tango, not fall and implore.

Let's melt away all this winter dread,
Replace hot cocoa with warm wedding spread.
If love's a fire, there's ice all about,
Bring on the sun, and let's hear love shout!

When Warmth Takes Flight

A penguin's dance upon the ice,
This chill sure doesn't feel quite nice.
As icicles form in my hair,
I'm just hoping for summer to be fair.

Birds fly south with all their might,
While I'm here wishing for warmth's sweet light.
Why must the heat take such a flight?
I'd barter my mittens for a beach delight.

Skating, slipping, oh what a fate,
Who knew romance could come with cold hate?
Frosty kisses, not my cup of tea,
Give me sunbathing, preferably by the sea.

So here's a toast, with hot cocoa sip,
To warmth returning on a sunny trip.
When the thaw comes, I will cheer and sing,
For warmth will return, like a flapping wing!

Navigating a Frosty Detour

Maps in winter are full of lies,
I trudge along, hoping for the skies.
This frosty path leads to nowhere,
A snowy detour with ice everywhere.

My nose is red, my cheeks aglow,
Each step I take, more ice I sow.
With every slip, it's laughter I find,
What a frosty joke the universe designed!

I was promised sun, bright rays and heat,
Instead, I'm skidding on frozen street.
A snowball fight? Oh, what a dream,
But planning it out is harder than it seems.

So here's to winter with all its flaws,
Let's dance with snow, take a chance on paws.
For through this frosty, slippery plight,
We'll navigate joy as though it's flight!

Chasing Sunlight Through Frozen Shadows

Chasing the sun feels like a game,
Through frozen shadows, who's to blame?
Each ray of warmth is a fleeting tease,
I find my joy in a chilly breeze.

Snowmen pop up with googly eyes,
While I daydream of warm burger fries.
Sledding sounds fun, but oh what a mess,
Frosty surprises cause much distress.

The warmth is near, but still far away,
I dress like a marshmallow, day after day.
When will this winter take a break?
Perhaps next week, for goodness' sake!

So let's giggle, let's chase the light,
Through all the frost, we'll take our flight.
With humor and warmth, we'll find our way,
Leaving winter's chill to a brightened day!

Unwilling Host to Winter's Grip

Snowflakes dance without a care,
While I'm trapped in layers, it's quite unfair.
My coffee's cold, my socks are wet,
Who knew this chill would be my threat?

The garden's dead, the flowers pout,
The trees in white, there's no doubt.
I signed up for warmth and sun,
But here I am, just come undone.

The snowman smiles, that cheeky chap,
While I just want to take a nap.
He wears my scarf, that crafty beast,
Stealing joy, to say the least!

Oh winter, you're a jolly foe,
With icy breath and cheeks aglow.
But when it ends, I'll turn the page,
And shake my fist in frosty rage!

Whispers of a Reluctant Season

Came November, wrapped in chill,
With frosty whispers, quite the thrill.
Yet here I sit, in toe socks bright,
Wishing for warmth, the sun outright!

The mittens laugh, they know my fate,
While I just ponder my sad state.
Hot cocoa dreams turn cold and gray,
As winter stages its grand play.

Chasing snowflakes, they taunt my hair,
"Oh dear, not another layer!"
Snow boots squish like a soggy pie,
At this rate, I might just cry!

Yet through the storm and the icy frown,
A giggle sneaks, can't keep me down.
So here's to warmth, when it returns,
For summer dreams, my heart still yearns!

Frosted Horizons of the Mind

Thoughts freeze solid, like old bread,
Questions linger, yet go unsaid.
Brr, it's chilly, my brain does freeze,
What did I sign up for? Oh, geez!

The sun hibernates, the wind just chides,
As I find comfort where warmth hides.
In fuzzy socks, I'm quite the sage,
But longing for sun, I'm still a page.

Coffee drips, its steam all gone,
A frosty veil, the shine withdrawn.
Must lounge by fire, best stay in bed,
Winter's grip is all in my head!

Oh frosty dreams, with hearts so bold,
Humor stirs in the bitter cold.
One day I'll laugh at all this bliss,
But until then, I'll simply hiss!

Shards of Unforeseen Ice

Icicles hang like tiny swords,
As I braved through outside hoards.
One slip, a slide, oh what a sight,
Making taco shapes, with all my might!

Snowballs whirl, they target me,
My laughter echoes, wild and free.
Oh, joyous war on winter's field,
Each frozen hit, my fate is sealed!

Frost bites hard, like a sneaky thief,
Yet here I am, with smiles, not grief.
I'll wear my hat like a crown so grand,
A jester's pomp on this icy land!

So raise a cup to the chill we face,
With snowflakes served on a silver plate.
For when spring bursts in with shining cheer,
We'll toast to frost, with laugh and beer!

Chill of Unexpected Mornings

Woke up today, oh what a shock,
My breath is visible, like a frozen clock.
Sipped my coffee, it's turned to ice,
Thought it was a brew, but now it's a slice.

Slippers on, feeling quite the fool,
Didn't know I'd skate to the bathroom school.
Checked the weather, it told me lies,
Forecast for sun, but I see white skies.

The dog looks at me like I've lost my mind,
Refusing to go out, he's sent back to find.
With snowballs and work, my mood takes a lift,
Who knew that morning could come with a gift!

Yet here I stand, wrapped up tight,
Laughing at winter, it's quite the sight.
If this is a joke, then count me in,
I'll dance with the frost, let the fun begin!

The Uninvited Winter Whisper

A fluffy intruder at my front door,
Came in with whispers, who asked for more?
My plants look worried, they're holding their breath,
"Decision quick, do we fight or accept death?"

The cats are plotting, a snowball attack,
While I'm inside, I'm wearing a snack.
With mittens and scarves, oh who wore them best?
Not me, as I trip, look at this wild fest!

A snowflake lands on my nose with glee,
As if it knows just how cold I could be.
"Stop being dramatic!" the postman will tease,
While I'm transformed into a human snow sneeze.

I'll spin around, like a frosty ballerina,
With each step a slip, I'm now a hyena.
The laugh is contagious, can't help but cheer,
Winter, dear winter, you've brought me such fear!

Frostbitten Dreams Awaken

Dreamt of beaches, the sun on my face,
Woke up instead, in a wintery embrace.
My warm thoughts shattered like glass on the floor,
Reality hits when you open the door.

The forecast was sunny, a summer delight,
Instead, I'm dodging the cold, what a fright!
The ice cream truck's muted, seems frozen in time,
While I'm here in layers, dancing in rhyme.

Hot cocoa's my weapon against this white foe,
But every sip tastes like a cruel winter blow.
Pjs turned icy, and socks on my hands,
I'm the king of a kingdom with fantastical plans.

Yet laughter erupts, as I slip and I slide,
In this winter wonderland, just take it in stride.
Let's build a snowman, give him a hat,
Even if it's hard, I'll have the last laugh at that!

Shivering in Surrender

Surrendered my sanity, now wrapped like a gift,
With thermals and blankets, oh, give me a lift!
Sipping hot tea while my toes just turn blue,
Wondering how cold I could possibly skew.

The neighbor's dog barks, a wintery cheer,
While I'm here looking like I've misplaced my rear.
Wobbling outside, all bundled like dough,
Each step is a gamble, each turn's quite the show.

"Tomorrow will melt all your icy heart,"
Said the weatherman, "That's just the start."
I grin as the snowflakes tease me with glee,
Tomorrow's bright promise is still a bit free.

With laughter and shivers, the cold can't be beat,
I'll take winter's charm while wearing my heat.
So here's to the snow that covers the ground,
In this frosty madness, it's joy that I've found!

The Surreal Season of Surprise

In the morning light, oh what a tease,
The ground is dressed in icy freeze.
I planned for sun, a picnic grand,
But here I stand, with snowball in hand.

My flip-flops scream, 'What a mistake!'
While frostbit toes begin to ache.
Who knew a stroll could turn so wild?
Cold cheeks laugh, like a silly child.

The trees are wearing coats of white,
In this comedy, where's the delight?
Snowflakes pirouette, a frosty dance,
Oh, how I wish for warm romance!

But here comes winter, with quirky cheer,
It seems to love this time of year.
To all who grumble, here's the jest:
Grab a sled, and let's all rest!

Snowfall's Reluctant Embrace

Outside my window, a flurry spins,
A frosty hug, where chaos begins.
My warm mug waits, but here's the catch,
The ground is slick; it's quite a match.

The snowmen grin with carrot noses,
In frozen poses, like silly roses.
I tripped on ice and landed with flair,
A comedy sketch; I could've sworn it was rare!

Around comes winter, dressed to the nines,
Whispering secrets in cold, funny lines.
I laugh through the chill, though my teeth may chatter,
Who needs summer when there's this funny matter?

So grab your mittens, put up a show,
While winter giggles, let's go with the flow.
A face full of snow, oh what a sight!
In winter's wonder, we frolic in light!

The Heart Versus the Cold

Heart's beating faster, it's icy outside,
In thick heavy coats, nowhere to hide.
Puffs of breath make clouds in the air,
As laughter escapes, tousled without care.

But warmth is a battle, I question my style,
With frozen fingers, it's been a while.
My heart wants flowers, yet snowflakes invade,
A love poem lost in winter's charade.

Yet somehow this chill, it brightens the heart,
In snappy encounters, we all play a part.
From snowball fights to cozy chats,
Love finds a way, like curious cats.

Though the frost bites down like a sneaky thief,
We'll dance through this season, beyond disbelief.
Toasty fires crackle, as hot cocoa pours,
In winter's embrace, who could ask for more?

Frost's Unwanted Visit

Well, look who's here, Mr. Frosty Gaze,
He strolled right in, all the wrong ways.
My plans for spring turned to icy dread,
As he settles in, my warm dreams fled.

Knocking at doors, he jangles my hair,
In a chilly whisper, 'Why should I care?'
With socks gone missing and coats piled high,
He's the uninvited guest, oh my, oh my!

Hot coffee steaming, with ice on the rim,
It's hard to pretend that the sun isn't dim.
The garden is tangled, all under his spell,
Each flower now frozen—a prank, can't you tell?

We laugh and we grumble, at the chilly facade,
While winter's antics become a charade.
So here's to the frost that gets in our way,
Let's dance in our boots, and fake a bright day!

Winter's Unscripted Turn

The snowflakes dance like they're on a spree,
My warm boots scream, "Let me be free!"
Hot cocoa's now my bestest friend,
While my patience melts like a snowman's end.

The squirrels wear coats, oh what a sight,
Planning heists to snatch snacks at night.
I wave to the ice, as it takes my car,
And wonder if winter's gone too far.

Each icicle's dangling, a comic sword,
Threatening heads like a playful horde.
My fingers are numb, but I've got a plan,
To lure some sunshine with a catchy jam.

Oh fluff of white, we jest and jive,
In this frosty circus, we'll all survive.
With laughter warm, we'll chase the chill,
As winter's antics give us a thrill.

Amidst Unexpected Chill

The forecast lied, it's snowing again,
My scarf's a tangled twist, oh what a sin!
Slipping and sliding, I'm quite the show,
As neighbors giggle, "Look at them go!"

Hot soup's my armor, oh so divine,
Yet it's hard to navigate between bites and brine.
The cat just sneezed; it looks unamused,
While I'm trapped in layers, thoroughly bruised.

The snowman I built looks slightly deranged,
With a carrot nose, but his smile's changed.
His twigs are waving, a friendly cheer,
"I feel your cold, but when's spring near?"

Amidst this chaos, I'll bake some pie,
With hope and warmth, we'll let winter fly.
So here's to the chill and the frosty fun,
For every iceberg melts when spring's begun!

An Uninvited Dance with Ice

Slipping on ice, oh what a freak,
I'm no dancer; I just feel weak!
The ground has turned into a slippery stage,
While laughter erupts like a musical page.

With every tumble, I take a bow,
The world is my audience, don't ask me how.
Frosty pirouettes, my skill set's a joke,
I'm hoping for warmth with each icy poke.

Footprints are stories, this path now a brew,
Of mishaps and giggles; oh, how they accrue!
Each step's an adventure, each turn a surprise,
I've perfected the art of winter's demise.

So bring on the chill, let's giggle and gleam,
In this frosty folly, it's all a dream.
What's life without laughter, a little ice-fall,
Let's dance with the snow till it blankets us all!

Echoes of a Shivering Soul

Frosty windows weave a tale tonight,
Of cold mischief making hearts ignite.
I put on my socks, three pairs, maybe four,
Yet somehow, I feel like I'm lost at sea shore.

Chattering chins, we huddle like cheese,
As friends trade hot tales over steaming teas.
My nose seems to host an adorable glow,
While winter's ensemble gives quite the show.

Laughter erupts at my flailing arms,
As I dodge snowflakes and extra farm charms.
Who knew that cold could be such a blast?
With giggles and shivers, we'll have a blast!

So here's to the frost; it'll come and it'll go,
But the memories made will always flow.
With a wink and a grin, we'll face every blight,
Echoes of laughter, through winter's own night.

Silent Tears on Frozen Soil

In a coat too tight, I stomp and slide,
My nose like Rudolph, my pride, denied.
The snowflakes dance, they laugh at me,
As I trip on frost and spill my tea.

Each breath I take, a cloud so white,
Winter's chill gives quite a fright.
With every step, a yelp escapes,
How can this be? I'm not in capes!

The ground is hard as frozen pie,
I'd trade it all for sunshine high.
Yet here I stand, in frozen gloom,
With silent tears, I grumble, fume.

But here's a twist; I found some cheer,
The squirrels are plotting! Oh dear, oh dear!
They mock my plight, it feels absurd,
Maybe I'll join them, and then be heard.

Crystal Chains That Bind

Ice-skates are not what they seem,
I slide around like in a dream.
If a penguin laughs, I might just cry,
Stuck in this snow, I wonder why.

My boots are anchored, full of snow,
With every step, I feel the woe.
I never thought I'd dance this way,
With crystal chains that won't decay.

Yet here I am, a frosty mess,
Trying to look like I'm stylish, yes.
But every twirl just earns a fall,
A winter wonderland's rise and sprawl.

Oh, winter's chill has turned me bold,
I'll strut my stuff through winters cold!
With every slip, I'll laugh and boast,
Here's to the chaos that I love most!

The Frost That Fell Where Grass Grew

Once lush and green, now pure white,
The grass is frozen, what a sight!
I thought I'd sunbathe, get a tan,
Instead, I'm tumbling, oh man, oh man!

My summer plans went right on freeze,
Now I'm battling a cold with sleaze.
I tried to jump over a mound,
But instead, I plunged in, oh how I drowned!

Impressions of penguins mark my track,
With frozen fingers, I'll not hold back.
A snowball fight? Yes, count me in!
Maybe I'll finally get a win!

So here's to frost on grass so green,
A wacky world, it must be seen.
With laughter ringing through the cold,
Winter's tales can be retold!

The Heartbeat Beneath a Winter Sky

Beneath this frost, I feel the thud,
My heart is racing, stuck in crud.
The snowman smiles, he's quite the host,
While I'm here wishing for summer most.

Yet winter's pulse is quirky, fun,
A snowflake dance, with laughter spun.
While jackets puff, like marshmallow foes,
With frozen limbs, we strike a pose.

Oh, what a show, this winter spree,
With every snowball, I giggle with glee.
The chill wraps tight, but so does cheer,
Beneath this sky, I've naught to fear.

So take my hand, let's glide anew,
With each cold breath, I'll laugh with you.
From frozen tears to joyous sighs,
Our joyous hearts light up the skies.

The Ice That Trapped My Heart

Last night my heart was quite the bouncer,
But now it's stuck, a frozen flouncer.
I tried to skate, thought I was slick,
But tripped on ice, felt like a brick.

A bird flew by, it couldn't help pause,
I caught its glare, it looked just because.
'What a cold day!' it chirped with a wink,
I laughed aloud, this ice made me think.

A snowman nearby looked quite bemused,
While my warm coffee was thoroughly bruised.
With frozen toes and a shivery grin,
I'll make a joke, let the fun begin!

So here I stand, with socks mismatched,
In layers of fluff, I'm slightly detached.
A heart once bold now needs a good thaw,
But it's a laugh, and that's quite the score!

Frozen Moments

The world is frosted, cars all stuck,
I slip and slide like a clumsy duck.
A frozen smile, my cheeks are red,
'Nice to meet you!'—to the ground I said.

Each laugh I shared went whoosh in the air,
Caught in a bubble, drifting somewhere.
Pine trees glisten like they are in awe,
I look like a snowman, but without the jaw!

With frosty tips on my favorite hat,
I danced to the tunes of a snowman chat.
And little birds, with coats that were bright,
Sang me a carol, oh what a sight!

But all this magic makes my lips blue,
While icicles poke my hair—just a few!
The jokes I tell might just be too chill,
But laughter is warmth, and that's the thrill!

Fleeting Hopes

I dreamed of spring in a frosty glade,
But trapped in ice, my dreams start to fade.
I cough on snowflakes, they're cold and rude,
Is this the season? I feel quite subdued.

Hopes flew by like snowflakes in flight,
Each wish seems frozen, out of my sight.
With every slip, I utter a cheer,
'This icy saga is perfectly clear!'

The sun may peek, oh, once or twice,
But clouds swoop in, it's like rolling dice.
I wave at passers, we share a frown,
What's fun about slipping on your own gown?

Yet laughter bubbles through the freeze,
As snowmen gather with such silly ease.
We dance around with visions of flair,
Fleeting hopes transform into frozen air!

Shadows in the Frost

My shadow dances on the ice so thin,
Looks like it's laughing, trying to win.
With every jig, I'm off my axis,
Beat by frost, what a silly practice!

The snowflakes giggle as they swirl around,
While I attempt to get off the ground.
'Hold on tight!' whispers the chilly breeze,
But instead, I slip, bringing down the trees!

Fun in the frost, like children we play,
Making snow angels and flinging away.
Yet I stumble through the white fluffy haze,
With shadows mocking in comical ways!

So here I remain, in this winter spree,
Lost in the laughter, my shadow's with me.
Frosty giggles and chilly delight,
Who needs warm thoughts when fun's in sight?

Too Many Layers, Not Enough Warmth

Bundled up tight in these layers galore,
Feeling like a burrito, can't take much more.
Each outfit stacked, a colorful fright,
But all I feel is a cold bit of bite.

Hands wrapped in mittens, they wiggle and dance,
Trying to wave but just lacking romance.
With leg warmers tied, and hats on so fun,
I'm puffy and rounded, not able to run.

Too many layers—am I ready for space?
Yet shivering still, it's a comical race.
In this chilly bluster, I trip and I fall,
Snow on my face, oh I'm loving it all!

So here is the truth, I may bumble and sway,
But laughter is warm on a winter's cold day.
With too many layers, I'll dance like a queen,
Embracing the chill, I'm the warmest in sheen!

The Day the Heat Gave Way

The sun decided to take a nap,
Leaving us in this chilly trap.
Sweaters on, we shiver and shake,
Dreaming of warmth, for goodness' sake.

Hot cocoa's now a daily delight,
But where's my sunscreen? Ain't that right?
The beach ball's still in the shed,
Next to my hopes of a tan instead!

Snowflakes dance like they own the show,
While we munch on popcorn, thoughts of 'no.'
Winter went rogue, created a mess,
And all I can do is laugh, I guess!

So here's to the heat that fled the scene,
Left us to freeze like a soggy bean.
We'll make the best of this chilly spree,
With scarves as our capes, watch us be free!

An Arrival in the Mists of Winter

One morning I woke to a shocking chill,
The warmth had vanished, what a bitter thrill.
Mittens and scarves now part of my attire,
My breath forms clouds, but I can't catch fire.

The snowman's not round, he's a total flop,
With arms that sag low, like a sleepy mop.
Snowball fights? More like slips and falls,
Winter's a prankster, laughing through walls.

Hot tea in hand, I dance with a grin,
While my toes are frozen, oh, where do I begin?
The dog's a snowball, rolling with glee,
But I just wanted a warm cup of tea!

Winter arrived with a chilly embrace,
But I'll weather the storm with a smile on my face.
So bring on the frost, let's take it in stride,
With laughter and cheer, we'll enjoy the ride!

Unwanted Frost on Starlit Wishes

Woke from my dreams, what's this outside?
A white blanket covering my sleepy pride.
Stars are twinkling in frosty delight,
But I'd rather be warm than freeze through the night.

My wishes were for a summer's glow,
Instead, I'm stuck in a winter show.
The neighbors are bundled, ready to fight,
Snowball wars echo under the streetlight.

With every gust that bites at my nose,
I realize my dreams are in frozen pose.
But laughter rings out, it fills up the air,
As we trip and tumble, not a single care.

So here's to the frost that came way too fast,
Turning our moments into a laugh that will last.
With joy in our hearts and snow on our toes,
We'll dance through the chill 'til the warm weather glows!

The Weight of Frosted Air

Each breath I take carries a small frost bite,
Why's it so heavy? I just want to write!
The air feels thick, like it's got a plan,
To turn my hot coffee into icy, cold can.

I step outside, my hair turns to icicles,
Someone please save me from these silly cycles.
The world is a postcard, but I'm stuck with a pen,
I'd trade in my frost for the warmth of a den!

Snow boots on, I waddle like a goof,
Laughter rings out—there's no other proof.
Frost on my face, what a sight to behold,
Yet I smile wide, never feeling old.

So yes, the air carries weight, that's true,
But with every step, we'll make our own view.
For winter may come with its cold, silly charade,
But together we shine, in laughter we're made!

A Journey Through Uncharted Frost

I ventured out, all dressed so neat,
But now my toes have faced defeat.
My hot cocoa's turned to icy slush,
As snowflakes dance in a winter hush.

The map said sunny, no snowflakes spied,
But here I am, like a penguin I slide.
My fingers freeze into a frosty mess,
This journey's charm? A big, cold guess!

With every step, I slip and slide,
My winter boots have lost all pride.
The snowman winks, he's got more grace,
While I perform in this laughable race.

I thought of fun in a winter spree,
Instead, I'm stuck in a chilly sea.
Oh, whims of weather, you sly, frosty cheat,
Tomorrow's plan? A retreat, elite!

Encased in a Winter's Grasp

Wrapped so tight in layers galore,
I look like a marshmallow fit to soar.
Each step I take, a crunch echoes loud,
As I wobble like a wintery crowd.

Hot chocolate's steaming, but I must confess,
It's lost all heat; now it's just a mess.
With my nose so red and cheeks aglow,
I can't help but laugh at my frozen show.

My breath creates clouds, like a dragon's flare,
While snowflakes fall, tickling my hair.
Oh frost, you tease with your chilly grin,
Next time I'll stick to a sunny spin!

In this frosty grip, I shiver and dance,
Each moment a chance for a clumsy romance.
So here I remain, encased without fear,
A frosty jester, that much is clear!

The Sudden Freeze of Desire

Just yesterday, I sought a warm breeze,
But now I'm trapped with the cold to tease.
My ambitions melted like ice cream fast,
As winter's chill threw a frosty blast.

I dreamt of sandy beaches, sun on my face,
But found a snowdrift, a cold, white embrace.
With every shiver, my plans seem to freeze,
What happened to warmth, oh winter, please tease!

My hot date's now a snowball fight,
We laugh till we cry, in the pale moonlight.
With frozen fingers, we try for a kiss,
But the chill outside makes it one frosty miss!

Oh sweet desire, how quickly you fade,
In the depths of winter, your plans are delayed.
I'll take this freeze with a chuckle and cheer,
Next time, dear weather, bring springtime near!

Frosted Alliances, Broken Trusts

My friends and I, we made a pact,
No snow would bind our winter act.
Yet here we stand, backs against the wall,
Our laughs now echoed by a slippery fall.

We planned a trip for hot cocoa and fun,
Instead we slid and stumbled, oh what a run!
Every attempt to walk straight and true,
Ends with laughter, and snowflakes anew.

Old alliances now thawed and split,
As one trips and the other has to admit,
That winter's power is a tricky jest,
We're bundled together, but not at our best!

So raise a toast to these frosty schemes,
With cups full of laughter and snowy dreams.
Though trust may slip on this icy floor,
We'll laugh all the more; can't wait for more!

Frosted Alliances, Broken Trusts

My friends and I, we made a pact,
No snow would bind our winter act.
Yet here we stand, backs against the wall,
Our laughs now echoed by a slippery fall.

We planned a trip for hot cocoa and fun,
Instead we slid and stumbled, oh what a run!
Every attempt to walk straight and true,
Ends with laughter, and snowflakes anew.

Old alliances now thawed and split,
As one trips and the other has to admit,
That winter's power is a tricky jest,
We're bundled together, but not at our best!

So raise a toast to these frosty schemes,
With cups full of laughter and snowy dreams.
Though trust may slip on this icy floor,
We'll laugh all the more; can't wait for more!

Shivering Under a Veil of White

In the morning light, oh so bright,
My breath is visible, such a fright!
Wrapped in layers, a snowy quilt,
Each step a shuffle, my toes can wilt.

The dog leaps high, a bounding sight,
Chasing snowflakes, what a delight!
But there I stand, frozen mid-laugh,
A snowman's rival in the cold bath.

Hot cocoa waits, a sweet embrace,
Yet still I linger, frozen in place.
This wasn't the plan, how did I misread?
Ice castles are real, my toes still plead.

Laughter echoes, in frosty air,
Friends throwing snowballs, life without care.
I giggle and shiver, so much to see,
What a wild world, this snow-draped glee!

A Walk Through Unexpected Glaciers

Stumbling through flakes like a dog on a slide,
Icicles hanging, my pride's set aside.
With each careful step, I panic and sway,
Who knew this winter would lead me astray?

Snowmen parade with noses of glee,
But here I am, stuck like a tree.
The air is so crisp, my cheeks feel alive,
Chasing down laughter, we must all survive.

Was it me, or did the sky conspire?
To blanket the world in this cold attire?
I step on the crust, it cracks with a pop,
In this frosty circus, I can't seem to stop.

But hey, at least the hot chocolate's near,
Worth the wild dance in the chilly frontier.
With friends by my side, who cares if I trip?
This snowy adventure is a joy-filled script!

Uneasy Cold in a Warm Heart

My heart is toasty, yet cold's at the door,
Caught in a swirl of the winter's big roar.
With mittens and scarves, I chuckle and frown,
How is it cold and I'm still dressing down?

The warmth of my soup is a comforting grace,
Yet the chill in my toes keeps a fast-paced race.
As I dance in the kitchen, just trying to heat,
The icy breeze whispers, 'You can't feel your feet!'

Flickering flames shimmer, they pull me in tight,
But the frosty whispers tell me, 'You're not quite right!'
I smile at the snowflakes, they play in the air,
Taunting my socks as if it were fair.

So here I stand, a warm little mess,
Winter giggles, oh what a jest!
Toasty inside, a frosty charade,
Wrapped in this fun, let my laughter cascade!

The Haze of Frosty Anticipation

Woke up this morning, what a sight unseen,
The world out my window, a glistening sheen.
What time is breakfast? Will the ice stay?
Pondering the chaos of this frosty play.

Frosted reminders cling to my nose,
I could stay in bed, but where's the pose?
Each dip in the path, a laugh and a scream,
This icy ballet, a winter's dream.

The garage door won't budge, it's a furious test,
Yet somehow it's funny, this bitter jest.
So grab that shovel, let's dance with the snow,
Turning mundane tasks into merry shows.

At last, I'll embrace this chill-filled charade,
With giggles and glee, the frosty parades.
This haze of anticipation, mixed laughter and cheer,
In a world dressed in white, every smile draws near!

Unforeseen Icicles of Discomfort

Thought I'd wear my summer shoes,
But here I am in winter blues.
My toes ached in a frosty dance,
Next time, maybe skip the chance.

A snowball fight turned into slips,
With icy landslides from my hips.
I aimed for fun, but lost my balance,
Now my laughter's lost in silence.

Hot cocoa's waiting, bitter sweet,
But first, let's rescue my frozen feet.
The world's a fridge, my face a pout,
Next year, summer's what it's about!

So here I stand, a frosty clown,
Wishing for a warmer town.
Turns out snow's not all delight,
Where's the sun? Oh, what a fright!

Frost-Edged Decisions

Woke up today with a chilly glee,
Should I wear a parka or just be free?
Deciding what to layer on right,
Ended up bundled, oh what a sight!

Muffler tight and gloves askew,
I look like a snowman in this view.
Dropped my scarf — oh what a fuss,
Now it's a sled for a daring bus!

Each step I take, a potential slide,
I'm a graceful penguin — with ice as my guide.
The path looks clear, but ice is sly,
With laughter and flailing, I wave goodbye!

Winter woes, they come on strong,
I'll just make jokes; can't go wrong.
Next summer, I'll plan a parade,
'Til then, it's snow and mischief made!

The Paradox of All Things Cold

Winter's chill in a sunny glance,
How'd I end up in this frigid dance?
Sweaters piled high, my mind's in a knot,
Thoughts of heat? Well, they've left the spot.

Pushed to the brink, in layers I bloat,
My little toes wish they could float.
Chasing snowflakes, I trip with a laugh,
Turns out, ice is no friendly half!

Breath clouding like secrets untold,
Why's it funny when it's so cold?
I chuckle at my own dismay,
But truly, who booked this winter's stay?

Once I wished for a snow-filled spree,
Now it's just me and the bitter freeze.
So here I am, amidst frozen grace,
Loving this winter, in a slippery race!

Cold Breath Under a Turning Sky

Under a sky that's shifting hues,
I swagger through with frosty shoes.
Every gust makes me gasp and grin,
Why would anyone choose to dive in?

Snowflakes swirl like confetti in flight,
While I shiver beneath the bright light.
A dance with the wind, rather absurd,
Who knew winter could be so disturb?

Hot soup awaits, but first a jog,
Footing's tricky—like hopping a frog.
I stumble and laugh, call it free art,
With every faceplant, I've found my heart!

As the sun sets on this chilly spree,
I wave free to warm memories.
Next winter, I'll sit by a fire bright,
Here's to embracing snow with delight!

Silent Crystals

Snowflakes dance on my nose,
I thought I'd skipped the winter woes.
My coffee's cold, what a surprise,
I see my breath, oh how it lies!

A snowman forms, but he looks bleak,
His carrot nose is a bit too meek.
Chasing warmth in this icy game,
Why's Mother Nature so full of shame?

Inside my house, the heater's off,
This chill's a real sneaky scoff.
Woolly socks upon my feet,
Yet here I am, feeling the sleet!

Where's the sun? A missed invite,
I'd trade my boots for sun-warmed light.
These frozen days are absurd but bright,
Like a comedy show, my own frosty plight.

Loud Heartbeats

In a chilly breeze my heart does race,
I dash inside to find my place.
With every beat, it calls aloud,
'This weather's weird, not fitting a crowd!'

With a scarf wrapped tight, I feel like a ball,
Waddling about, I might just fall.
Ice on the ground is all around,
I'm shuffling like I'm on shaky ground!

Outside the window, the world's a show,
With slips and trips like a comedy pro.
Heartbeats sync with the ice's crack,
Will I survive this heart-worn track?

Laughter erupts at my snowy stride,
Friends point and giggle, oh, what a ride!
A heart so loud can find the fun,
In winter's chill, we laugh as one.

The Cold Shoulder of Fate

Woke up this morn, feeling fresh and bright,
But fate gave me frost, not warm sunshine light.
With a shiver and shake, I exit my door,
Why does winter have to keep score?

My plans were for picnics, sun-soaked and sweet,
But ice-capped sidewalks shuffled my feet.
Hot chocolate dreams, but ice on my brow,
Why'd I wear shorts? I'm asking you now!

Fate's got a sense of humor so cold,
Turning warm weekends to frosty old gold.
Yet I laugh, as I slip on the floor,
With the cold shoulder, who could ask for more?

So here's to the chill, and all of its tricks,
My heart's still warm, feeling the kicks.
We'll dance through the ice, with giggles galore,
It's a fiasco of fun, who could want more?

A Winter's Bite Too Late

A winter's tale bit hard and quick,
Did I just hear a snowball trick?
Late in the game, this chill appears,
Stumbling out in shorts and cheers!

With mittens lost, and boots that squeak,
I venture forth, slightly less chic.
A leap, a slide, and down I go,
Oh, the drama of winter's show!

Snowflakes swirl like confetti on air,
My smile's bright, though I'm unaware.
A snowman built, with an artful flair,
Why's my nose so cold? I just don't care!

Chasing the dog who leaps with delight,
I stumble and tumble, what a fine sight!
In a world of frost, let laughter ignite,
The winter's bite is a comical fright!

Echoes of a Sudden Freeze

One moment sun, the next it's chill,
What's this tempest against my will?
Hoping for warmth; my shorts are a joke,
Now I'm a fun snowman, oh, that's my poke!

Echoes of freezing with every slip,
I'm like a penguin on a frosty trip.
Giggles erupt, as I lose my grace,
It's just me and ice in a wild race!

Frosty air plays hide and seek,
Catch my breath; laughter's peak.
With each icy blast, a funny scene,
Winter's comedy, a frosty routine.

So here's to the freeze that took us all,
In humorous moments, we take the fall.
With echoes of laughter that fill the space,
Embracing the chill is our warmest embrace.

Glacial Patterns of Regret

I thought it was just a light dusting,
But now I've built a whole snowman.
My plans melted like the sun's trusting,
Where am I hiding my warm tan?

Socks are soaked, and mittens are wet,
I lost my car in a snowdrift maze.
Who knew the forecast was a safe bet,
Now I'm stuck in this winter haze?

Each snowflake falls like taunts from fate,
Wishing for beaches and sunny skies.
Instead, I'm slipping on icy plate,
Oh, life's such a frozen surprise!

Hot cocoa's here, my glass is full,
But marshmallows keep floating away.
Winter's prankster, the humor's cruel,
Where's my sun? Oh, what a dismay!

Shattered Warmth

I bundled up with five layers thick,
But still felt the chill through the seams.
My toes are frozen, it's quite a trick,
Where's the warmth? Could it be dreams?

The heater's broken, what a laugh,
At least I've got my funny hat.
I'll dance in place, it's my own craft,
The winter blues? Just a silly chat.

Hot tea steams, a lovely sight,
But spills are common when cold winds blow.
Every drop's a winter bite,
Still laughing, oh, how they flow!

When snowflakes tumble and play tag,
I swing my arms, a playful flair.
With frozen cheeks, I must not brag,
But every laugh defies the air!

Crystal Ashes

Each morning greets me with icy breath,
As frost clings tight to the windowpane.
My shoes are caked; it feels like death,
I swear it's winter's cruel game.

Snow angels? More like frosty sharks,
Each fall's a comedy without a stage.
I laugh out loud, but it leaves marks,
Winter's humor? Truly all the rage!

Pine trees glisten in sparkly wear,
While I'm tumbling in cottony drifts.
Challenge accepted; it's only fair,
That nature brings me all these gifts.

Last night's chill was quite the tease,
Dreaming of warmth, but what a fight.
I'll fashion a snow fort with ease,
And toast to my victory tonight!

Frigid Surprises on a Winter's Eve

The snow fell gently, like dreams unreal,
I stepped outside—my fate was sealed.
But crickets chirping on icy wheels,
This evening's chilly, what a deal!

I brought my hot chocolate, spilled it wide,
Adventure called but I missed the text.
Now I'm laughing at the great divide,
As snowflakes dance, what's next?

The crunch beneath my clumsy boots,
Plays the symphony of frosty cheer.
Each shiver's a knock, my warmth dilutes,
Yet laughter echoes, crystal clear.

So here I stand, a frosty mess,
With a grin, I'll take this winter path.
For every flake that may distress,
Will only lead to a hearty laugh!

Layers of Glistening Uncertainty

What's hiding under all this white?
Might be snow, or a shoe from last fall.
Each step is a guessing game of fright,
 Will it stick, or just make me stall?

My hat's tipped back like a snowman's crown,
 As laughter dances on icy lips.
 In this winter play, I can't frown,
Though the chill might test my wits and grips.

Beneath the layers, a sandwich waits,
 Buried like treasure, forgotten long.
 Each bite brings joy, my heart elates,
 Winter's kitchen sings a silly song.

So let the frost provide its flair,
 In every mishap, I find the glee.
With giggles shared on this cold affair,
Life's fun when it's sprinkled with spree!

Beneath the Crystal Veil

Woke up today, what a sight to see,
A blanket of white, not a single tree.
My coffee's gone cold, the ice has me trapped,
There's snow in my slippers, my sanity's hapless.

The dog's making snowballs, oh what a delight,
He brings them inside, with a mischievous bite.
I thought we were just taking a stroll,
Now I'm chasing him down, losing all control.

The mailman appears as a snowman today,
His beard's frozen solid, he's lost in the play.
I wave through the window, then slip on the floor,
The ice in my drink is now less than a score.

So here's to the winter, this frosty affair,
I shiver and giggle while pulling my hair.
A snowman outside, a snowstorm in thought,
Next year, I'll be ready—oh wait, I forgot!

Interrupted by Snowflakes

Was just minding business, on my comfy chair,
Then suddenly snowflakes danced through the air.
They thought it was fun, I thought it was rude,
To cover my snacks—such a frosty food feud.

A snowflake's allure is a devilish tease,
It taunts from outside, like a chill in the breeze.
My hot cocoa's steaming, oh, the perfect brew,
But it froze in the air, like it knew what to do.

The roads have turned white, and the cars are so slow,
I peer out the window, my patience a no-show.
Penguins are sliding, on their merry old way,
While I'm in my PJs, just wanting to play.

So as I indulge in this frosty charade,
I can't help but laugh, as the snow's on parade.
Next year I'll protest, with my hot coffee stew,
For snow's not my friend, though it welcomes me too!

An Uninvited Guest at Dawn

Awoke to a crunch that was not quite a song,
A visitor crept in, thought it wouldn't be long.
It painted my car, left a trail of dismay,
An uninvited guest who just wouldn't obey.

I stumbled to greet it, a shovel in hand,
But each flake was stacked like an unplanned band.
My neighbors stand guard, armed with tea and their scrolls,
Declaring today's exercise, like fitness for souls.

The snowman's a joker, with a hat that won't fit,
He squints from the sunlight, giving me the bit.
We traded our worries, I promised him hot soup,
But then he just melted—oh, what a bad scoop!

As the sun sets the scene, my heart's light and spry,
For winter's a prankster, a trickster on high.
With laughter and snowflakes my worries take flight,
Though next time I'll set bounds, come the cold of the night!

The Frosty Grip of Fate

It started out normal, just me and my socks,
Then winter declared it: 'How about some frocks?'
A chill hit the room with a wallop of cheer,
As snowflakes took aim, oh, what a wild year!

At first it was fluff, just a sprinkle of glee,
But soon it wasn't quite how I thought it would be.
Each step to the door felt like climbing a hill,
My breath now a cloud, my wardrobe's goodwill!

The cat had a fit, went out for a look,
He'll be tracking in snow like a famous old crook.
With paw prints like art, he'll claim what is mine,
And laugh all the way, while I dance on the line.

So here's to the chill, and the laughter it brings,
Perhaps in this madness, we learn to wear wings.
With snow on my nose, and a smile on my fate,
I'll celebrate winter, oh what a fun state!

Uncharted Cold Realities

In socks that mismatch, I tread with care,
The chill creeps in like it just don't care.
My coffee mug wears a frosty coat,
I'm fumbling with mittens; it's hard to gloat.

The car won't start; it's a frozen tease,
I swear it's plotting this winter squeeze.
With layers like onions, I step outside,
My breath turns to clouds—oh, this is a ride!

The world's a white canvas, but wait a sec,
I'm slipping and sliding—what the heck!
The snowman I built is a lumpy mound,
My scarf's wrapped so tight, I can barely sound.

So let's celebrate this unpredictable chill,
With hot cocoa sipped while we attempt the drill.
Though winter's a prankster, I chuckle and grin,
With mittens and laughter, we all can win!

When Snowflakes Drift Without Warning

The forecast was sunny, or so I was told,
But here comes the snow, oh, the irony bold!
With hair like a yeti, I step through the door,
This surprise from the sky, I can't help but snore.

Just yesterday's shirt, so dry and so neat,
Is now hidden under this white, icy sheet.
Watch me trip over snowdrifts, oh, what a sight!
It's a wintery circus; my balance takes flight.

The dog in the yard thinks it's a grand game,
While I'm just stuck here, feeling quite lame.
Those rosy-cheeked kids toss snow in the air,
They laugh and they yell, without a single care.

Yet here I am, wishing for warmth once more,
The ice-cold breeze sneaks right through my door.
What happened to spring, this isn't my wish,
But hey, at least today I can't feel my fish!

Abrupt Winter's Caress

From beach to the blizzard, what a strange shift,
A snowball in hand instead of a gift.
I planned for a tan, maybe ice cream delight,
But here comes the flurries, oh what a fright!

Bundled like a turkey, I bumble and clatter,
The world's turned to crystals; it just doesn't matter.
With each step I take, I wobble and fall,
At this rate, I'll win the best tumble award!

The snowman is crooked, his arms made of twigs,
My hat's blown away; it's a disaster of digs.
Laughter erupts as I slip on my rear,
Don't mind me, folks—I'm just spreading the cheer!

So let's dance through the cold with our clumsy parade,
In a winter wonderland, we'll never fade.
With giggles and snowflakes, we'll brighten the day,
This icy surprise, it's a comical play!

The Frigid Surprise at Dawn

Awoke to a world that shimmered and glowed,
Jacket left hanging, I forgot it—oh no!
Fluffy boots on my feet, are they really for me?
I'll just take one step, what's the worst that could be?

With a crunch underfoot, I'm suddenly aware,
That the ground is a slip 'n slide—oh, do beware!
The mailbox is buried, my car's lost the race,
And now I'm just wishing to hibernate this space.

My neighbors are out, with shovels galore,
Chirpy and happy while I'm stuck on the floor.
A snowball flies past me—oh, what a surprise!
A wintertime whale, I'm dodging with sighs!

So here's to the frolic, the laughter, the cheer,
Though the frost bites my nose, I won't shed a tear.
For every cold morn has its quirky delight,
And every white wonder transforms wrong into right!

Silent Crystals on Troubled Ground

Crystals dance upon the grass,
With silent giggles, they pass.
Each blade shivers, a laugh takes flight,
Who thought winter could be so bright?

My toes numb, they squawk and squeal,
Sudden stomp on ice, oh what a deal!
A slip, a slide, a ballet of woes,
Never knew snow had such zany flows.

The trees don hats, all dressed to play,
I watch them gossip in a frosty ballet.
Snowflakes tumble, with charm they boast,
While I chase them down, a hapless host.

Yet in this chill, laughter still beams,
Cold air doesn't chill our silly dreams.
With ice and giggles, we plow ahead,
A winter wonderland, where joy is spread.

The Weight of Unwelcome Chill

Oh, what a weight this chill has brought,
Like stepping on Legos, I forgot!
The door creaks open, the breeze shoots in,
Winter's grip feels like an ice-cold grin.

With every shiver, my teeth do chatter,
Was it frost or my frazzled scatter?
A cup of cocoa, but it never warms,
These frozen antics transform my charms.

The snowman smiles with no carrot nose,
He's gone rogue with a hat from the throws.
Each breath a cloud in this frosty game,
Yet here we are, still laughing, all the same.

Beneath the chill, we forge our fun,
Embracing winter's mischief, one by one.
So here we stand, a laugh and a sigh,
With chilly jests, we'll reach for the sky.

Sudden Frost Upon Heartstrings

Frosty fingers tickle my heart,
A sudden chill, winter's sneaky art.
Socks mismatched, I stumble and trip,
On icy patches, my fate starts to flip.

Hot cocoa spills—oh, what a sight!
Marshmallow clouds in a frosty fight.
With sheepish grins, we clean the floor,
Who knew winter could open such doors?

A whisper of snowflakes tugs at my sleeve,
While winter's wildness plays tricks, I believe.
An orchestra of shivers plays our tune,
As snowmen plot under the big, bright moon.

So here's to the chill, the laughs that ensue,
On unexpected journeys, we dance like fools.
With bated breath, we embrace the gleam,
Winter's a jest; it's a whimsical dream.

Beneath Unfamiliar Winter Skies

Beneath these skies, a frosty frown,
Giggles echo in the snow-covered town.
Icicles dangle like teeth of a grin,
Who knew winter could let the laughter in?

My nose is red, like a ripe cherry,
Each gust of wind feels light and merry.
With snowball flurries and silliness rife,
We bumble through this cold, comical life.

Chasing snowmen as they skedaddle,
With frosty tails, they giggle and prattle.
I shiver and shake, but oh what a show,
In this unexpected, icy tableau.

So raise a mug to this chilled delight,
With mischief and fun, we'll take winter's bite.
In laughter and warmth, let's find our way,
Through frosty whims of a winter's day.

Where Warmth Used to Dwell

In my cozy chair, I sat so fine,
Sipping hot cocoa, feeling divine.
Then came a chill, what a surprise,
Now I'm wrapped up like a burrito, oh my!

My fuzzy socks have lost their charm,
As I hobble around, seeking warmth and calm.
The cat laughs loud, as I slide and slip,
What happened to sunny days? Oh, that's it—a blip!

Against a Wall of Ice

Out my window, a wonderland,
But it's stuck on freeze, it's way out of hand.
I'm battling icicles, sharp as a knife,
Who knew frozen chaos would bring new life?

I tried to skate, but my feet went astray,
Gliding like Bambi, in a comedic ballet.
Where's the control? Did it vanish in air?
Rolling downhill, with not a single care!

The Surprising Breath of Winter

Breath of fresh chill, it tickles my nose,
Did I sign for this? No one knows, I suppose.
Frosty exhalations dance all around,
Turning my laughter to ice with a sound.

Every step's a trap, oh what a tease,
Wishing for warmth as I wobble on knees.
Snowflakes are falling, making quite the scene,
A winter comedian, I've turned into keen!

Glistening Regrets in a Frosty Field

Oh look at the shine, it's quite a delight,
Till you step forward, and it takes flight.
Glistening regrets, do they come in a pack?
One slip on the ice, and it's all off track!

Building snowmen is a jolly old task,
But they keep melting, I dare not ask.
Do they have plans I don't understand?
While I trudge back home, feeling quite bland.

Milton Keynes UK
Ingram Content Group UK Ltd.
UKHW020741221124
451186UK00024B/180